Patrick Henry

*American Statesman
and Speaker*

Colonial Leaders

Lord Baltimore *English Politician and Colonist*

Benjamin Banneker *American Mathematician and Astronomer*

William Bradford *Governor of Plymouth Colony*

Benjamin Franklin *American Statesman, Scientist, and Writer*

Anne Hutchinson *Religious Leader*

Cotton Mather *Author, Clergyman, and Scholar*

William Penn *Founder of Democracy*

John Smith *English Explorer and Colonist*

Miles Standish *Plymouth Colony Leader*

Peter Stuyvesant *Dutch Military Leader*

Revolutionary War Leaders

Benedict Arnold *Traitor to the Cause*

Nathan Hale *Revolutionary Hero*

Alexander Hamilton *First U.S. Secretary of the Treasury*

Patrick Henry *American Statesman and Speaker*

Thomas Jefferson *Author of the Declaration of Independence*

John Paul Jones *Father of the U.S. Navy*

Thomas Paine *Political Writer*

Paul Revere *American Patriot*

Betsy Ross *American Patriot*

George Washington *First U.S. President*

Patrick Henry

*American Statesman
and Speaker*

JoAnn A. Grote

Arthur M. Schlesinger, jr.
Senior Consulting Editor

Chelsea House Publishers

Philadelphia

Dedication: For my niece, Alyssa Falvey

Produced by 21st Century Publishing and Communications, Inc.
New York, NY. http://www.21cpc.com

CHELSEA HOUSE PUBLISHERS
Editor in Chief Stephen Reginald
Production Manager Pamela Loos
Director of Photography Judy L. Hasday
Art Director Sara Davis
Managing Editor James D. Gallagher

Staff for *PATRICK HENRY*
Project Editor/Publishing Coordinator Jim McAvoy
Assistant Editor Anne Hill
Associate Art Director Takeshi Takahashi
Series Design Keith Trego

The Chelsea House World Wide Web address is
http://www.chelseahouse.com

First Printing
1 3 5 7 9 8 6 4 2

Library of Congress Cataloging-in-Publication Data

Grote, JoAnn A.
Patrick Henry / by JoAnn A. Grote.
80 pp. cm. — (Revolutionary War Leaders series)
Includes bibliographical references and index.
Summary: A biography of Patrick Henry, the Virginia lawmaker and
politician known for his stirring speeches and eloquent writing.
ISBN 0-7910-5357-1 (hc)   ISBN 0-7910-5700-3 (pb)
1. Henry, Patrick, 1736-1799—Juvenile literature. 2. Legislators—
United States—Biography—Juvenile literature. 3. United States—
Continental Congress—Biography—Juvenile literature. 4. Virginia—
Politics and government, 1775-1783—Juvenile literature. 5. United
States—Politics and government, 1775-1783—Juvenile literature.
[1. Henry, Patrick, 1736-1799. 2. Legislators.]   I. Title. II. Series.
E302.6.H5G76   1999
973.3'092—dc21   99-33135
[B]   CIP

Publisher's Note: In Colonial and Revolutionary War America, there were no standard rules for spelling, punctuation, capitalization, or grammar. Some of the quotations that appear in the Colonial Leaders and Revolutionary War Leaders series come from original documents and letters written during this time in history. Original quotations reflect writing inconsistencies of the period.

Contents

When Patrick Henry was a boy, most of the countryside
was covered with trees. Patrick loved to hunt animals
and listen to birds in the woods.

A New Voice

Did you ever get in trouble for saying what you believed? Are you ever afraid to say what you believe because people might not like it?

Patrick Henry said what he believed. He said what he believed to judges and rich people and lawmakers. He said what he believed even when he knew the king of England wouldn't like it.

Patrick expressed his opinions even when people in America could be put in prison for saying what they believed.

The things Patrick said made many Americans decide to fight in the Revolutionary War. His words helped other people feel brave. After the war his words reminded people not to give up the rights that so many people had fought so hard to win.

Some people became Revolutionary War heroes because they were brave soldiers, like George Washington. Some became heroes because they were brave spies, like Paul Revere. Patrick became a Revolutionary War figure because of the words he wrote and the way he spoke them.

But Patrick didn't start out a Revolutionary War hero. He started out just like you and me and everyone else—as a baby.

On May 29, 1736, Patrick caused quite a stir. He'd just arrived in the world. He was born at home, like all babies in the 1700s. Everyone in the house was excited to meet him.

Patrick's parents named him after his uncle, Reverend Patrick Henry. Most people called the older man **Parson** Henry because he was a pastor in the **Episcopal** church. They called the baby Patrick.

There were lots of people to welcome Patrick. He was born on a tobacco **plantation** called Studley in Virginia. Virginia was not a state yet. It was a **colony** of Britain at that time. Already Patrick had two brothers–John and William. John was Patrick's stepbrother. William and Patrick had the same parents.

The Henrys weren't the only people living at Studley. Many African-American slaves lived at Studley, too. Some of the slaves helped Patrick's father work the tobacco fields. Some of them helped Patrick's mother with house-work and cooking. They also helped care for Patrick and William and John.

When Patrick was still little a baby sister was born. And then another and another. Finally, Patrick had seven sisters.

Patrick was a skinny boy with reddish-brown hair. He was quiet sometimes. But he liked to have a good time. The plantation was a fun place for a boy to grow up. Patrick loved to play in the woods and by the river. He liked to play jokes on his friends, too.

Sometimes Patrick and his friends paddled canoes on the river. One day while canoeing, he talked them into going swimming. Then he hurried to be the first one out of his clothes. As he jumped into the river, he tipped over the canoe. His friends and their clothes all got dunked.

Sometimes Patrick didn't feel like playing, so he fished. He sat quietly for hours waiting for the fish to bite. While he waited, he listened. He listened to the river splashing along. He could hear the **cicadas** buzzing in the trees.

He listened to the birds, too. There were blue jays, cardinals, robins, sparrows, mockingbirds, whippoorwills, and crows. He wanted to learn the language of the birds. Patrick practiced copying the sounds they made.

Birdsongs weren't the only kind of music Patrick liked. He learned how to play the violin. One day he broke his collarbone. He couldn't play outside as he usually did. Instead of complaining, Patrick taught himself to play the flute.

Fishermen use long nets to catch fish in a river. Patrick liked to fish. Sometimes he and his friends liked to canoe and swim in the river, too.

As a boy, he also learned to hunt and trap. The forests around Studley were filled with game: deer, red foxes, wolves, turkeys, squirrels, raccoons, possums, and rabbits. Hunting became one of Patrick's favorite things to do. A friend said that Patrick was "fond of reading," "very fond of math," and "remarkably fond of his gun."

Patrick's father was a busy man. He not only ran the plantation but also was a judge. And he was a major in the **militia**. Patrick must have been proud of his father. When Mr. Henry went to the Hanover County Courthouse to act as a judge, he was dressed like a gentleman. He wore fine jackets, knee-length breeches, and a fancy, powdered wig.

The county's militia met near the courthouse on **muster** days. People gathered to watch them practice marching and shooting. Patrick's father marched in front, giving orders.

Young Patrick couldn't play and watch the militia all the time. He also went to school. First he went to a small neighborhood school. There he learned to read and write.

When Patrick was 10, Mr. Henry started teaching Patrick and William at home. Sometimes Parson Henry helped too. Patrick and William learned more about English and math. They also learned history, geography, Greek, and Latin.

What else did Patrick learn? He said Parson Henry taught him "[t]o be true and just in all my dealings. To bear no malice nor hatred in my heart. To keep my hands from picking and stealing. Not to covet other men's goods: but to learn and labor truly to get my own living, and to do my duty in that state of life unto which it shall please God to call me."

Mr. Henry and his brother Parson Henry were knowledgeable and were good teachers. They had gone to a university in Scotland. In those days most men never went to college.

Like most people, Patrick and his family went to church every Sunday. They might have to pay a **fine** if they didn't go. They might also have to pay fines if they didn't pay taxes to support the churches. The law said everyone had to go to the Episcopal church.

Patrick's mother didn't like the Episcopal church. She went to another church, even though it was against the law. So did Patrick's grandfather. Patrick's father was the judge. He had no choice but to fine Patrick's grandfather.

Patrick didn't think the law was right. He thought people should be able to go to any church they liked.

Mrs. Henry took the children to the church she liked. Patrick drove the carriage to church for his mother over the rutted red clay roads between tall trees.

The boy listened closely to the sermons. He knew his mother would ask him to repeat them on the way home. He didn't mind listening. In fact, Patrick found it hard not to listen. The pastor was Reverend Samuel Davies. He was one of the best speakers in America.

Patrick didn't just repeat the words of the sermon. He copied the way Reverend Davies said them. At times he spoke so softly that his mother and sisters could barely hear him. Other words he spoke very loudly. Sometimes he paused so the listeners could hardly wait for what he would say next. Other times he flung a fist into the air and threw his head

A church in colonial America. Patrick went to a church where Reverend Samuel Davies gave inspiring sermons. Patrick learned to be a great speaker by copying Reverend Davies.

back for emphasis. Another moment he let his shoulders slump.

When Patrick was an old man he told his grandson that he had learned to be a great speaker from watching Reverend Davies.

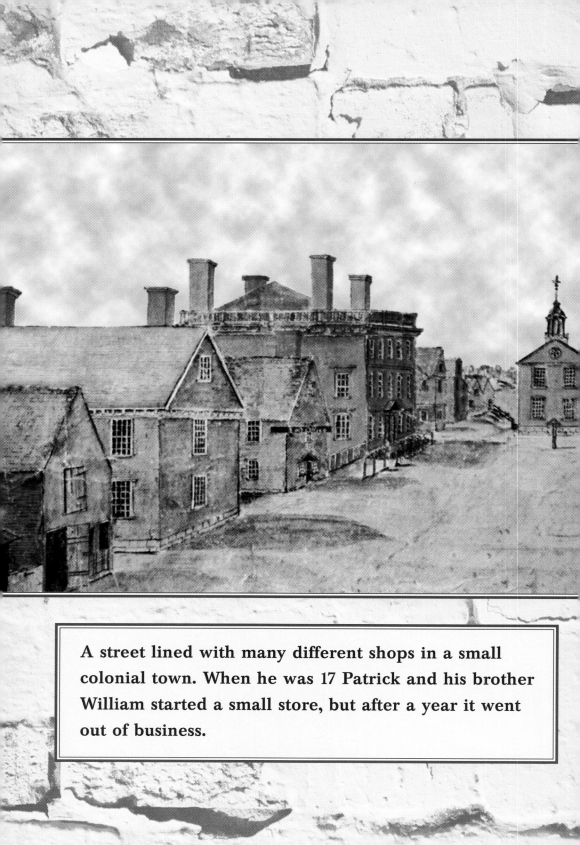

A street lined with many different shops in a small colonial town. When he was 17 Patrick and his brother William started a small store, but after a year it went out of business.

2

At the Frontier's Edge

The Studley plantation didn't belong to Mr. Henry. It belonged to Mrs. Henry's first husband. When he died, it went to Mrs. Henry—but only until their son, John, was old enough to run the plantation.

In 1749, when Patrick was 13, John became the owner of Studley. Patrick and his parents and his other brothers and sisters moved. They went to another plantation 20 miles away called Mount Brilliant. Twenty miles was a long way in the 1700s. It took a day for them to travel to Mount Brilliant.

Things were different in that part of Virginia.

There were more hills. Plantations were smaller. There weren't as many towns and fancy houses. People lived more simply.

Patrick liked it at Mount Brilliant. There were more woods around it than there were around Studley. He would explore the woods listening to birds and talking back to them. And there was another river where he could swim and fish and canoe.

Patrick did not live at Mount Brilliant very long, however. Everything changed when he was 15. His school years with his father ended. Now it was time for Patrick to decide what he would do when he became a man.

Most boys who learned Greek and Latin went to college. But knowing Greek and Latin didn't help Patrick. There was only one college in Virginia, the College of William and Mary, and his father couldn't afford to send him there.

Instead, Patrick spent a year learning to be a store clerk. Then Mr. Henry helped Patrick and William start their own small country store.

The store was set up near Studley. Patrick and William moved back to Studley and lived with their brother, John. Their customers were their old neighbors. Their friends would visit with them when they came to shop at the store.

Many of their customers were poor. Patrick and William would let the customers have what they needed. The customers promised to pay when they had enough money. Patrick would write down the amount of money they owed in his book. Many of the customers often weren't able to pay the money they'd promised, so Patrick and William didn't have money to buy more things for the store.

After a year Patrick and William closed the store. William moved west. But not Patrick—he had fallen in love.

The girl he loved was Sarah Shelton. Patrick called her Sallie. She was 16 and he was 18. Patrick had known her most of his life. Her father owned a tavern across the street from the Hanover Courthouse, where Mr. Henry was a judge. Sallie's grandfather was an important man to the people in Virginia. He had started Virginia's newspaper, the *Virginia Gazette,* the year Patrick was born.

In October 1754 Patrick and Sallie were married in the parlor at Sallie's home. Parson Henry performed the wedding ceremony. After the wedding, there was food and dancing for the guests. The celebrating went on for many days.

It was custom then when a girl married for her father to give a **dowry**. This meant the father gave a gift or sum of money to the man his daughter married. Sallie's father gave Patrick a farm and six African-American slaves. The farm was called Pine Slash. It was only half a mile from Sallie's parents' house.

Pine Slash wasn't a large plantation like Studley. The land wasn't as good for growing tobacco. Patrick worked with the slaves in the fields. They plowed the land, planted the crops, hoed weeds, and picked worms off the plants. In the fall they picked the strong-smelling tobacco leaves and

The first printing press in America. The grandfather of Patrick's wife, Sallie, started Virginia's newspaper, the *Virginia Gazette*, in 1736.

hung them up to dry. It was hard work.

All that hard work didn't produce much money for Patrick and Sallie. During the first summer at Pine Slash, there just wasn't enough rain and the tobacco didn't grow very well.

An early tobacco plantation. Tobacco was an important crop to Patrick on his little farm. It was also the basis for his first important case as a lawyer.

Patrick and Sallie's first child was born that summer. She was a baby girl. They named her Martha but called her Patsy.

Two years later there was a terrible accident, and their house burned down. Patrick sold some slaves for money to rebuild the house. A son named John was born that year. Then Patrick opened another store. He hoped that with a store and the farm he could support his family. He sold lots of things at the store: shoes, pocket knives, candle molds, salt, cloth, and hairpins.

But in 1759 there was another drought. Again Patrick's crops didn't grow well. Neither did his neighbors' crops. They couldn't pay for the things they bought at Patrick's store. Patrick and Sallie couldn't pay their bills, so they moved to town. They stayed at Sallie's father's tavern.

The years Patrick spent as a storekeeper and farmer were hard years. Patrick kept hoping things would get better. Later he wrote to a friend that "adversity toughens manhood." He meant that hard times make a person stronger.

At Christmastime Patrick and Sallie went to parties. Patrick liked to dance. Sometimes he played his flute or fiddle so others could dance. At a Christmas party in 1759, Patrick met a man who would be very important in America's future. His name was Thomas Jefferson.

Things were about to change for Patrick.

Williamsburg, the largest town in colonial Virginia, was also the capital of Virginia. Patrick rode 50 miles to Williamsburg to take his test to become a lawyer.

3

Patrick's Test

Jefferson was only 17 when Patrick met him. Patrick was 23. Many years later Jefferson wrote about meeting Patrick: "His manners had something of coarseness in them; his passion was music, dancing, and pleasantry. He excelled in the last, and it attracted every one to him."

Jefferson was on his way to college. He was studying to be a lawyer.

Patrick's father was a judge. And now his brother, John, became a judge too. Patrick decided he also wanted to be a lawyer. He still couldn't afford college, but he could read. He studied two law books. That wasn't enough to make him a lawyer. Before he could say he was a lawyer he had to pass a test.

People didn't take written tests to become lawyers in Virginia in the 1700s. Instead, two people who were already lawyers talked to the person who wanted to become a lawyer and asked him many questions about the law. If the two lawyers thought the questions were answered well, the person passed. Then he became a lawyer.

Patrick Henry rode his horse 50 miles to take his test. He rode over bumpy red clay roads and crossed many streams. Finally, he reached Williamsburg. Williamsburg was the biggest, most important town in Virginia. It was also the capital of Virginia. There were more than 200 houses in Williamsburg, many of them made of red bricks.

The College of William and Mary was the first place Patrick saw. He stopped there to visit Thomas Jefferson. Then he went to see the first

Thomas Jefferson, the second governor of Virginia and the third president of the United States. Thomas and Patrick became friends as young men and later worked together for freedom during the Revolutionary War.

lawyer. After the test the lawyer signed a paper saying Patrick had passed it.

Mr. Randolph was the next lawyer Patrick

went to see. He didn't think Patrick looked much like a lawyer because Patrick was dressed in simple clothes. And his clothes were very dirty and wrinkled from traveling on horseback for two long days.

The test took hours. Mr. Randolph asked Patrick many questions. He was surprised Patrick had only read two books. He took Patrick into his office and showed him his shelves lined with law books. "You have never seen any of these books," he scolded Patrick, "yet you are right and I am wrong." Mr. Randolph wisely suggested Patrick read more law books. But Patrick had passed the test.

After that Patrick became a lawyer. He could not stay in one place all day, like a storekeeper or a farmer. Instead, he traveled many miles to six different courthouses. Most of the time he rode his horse. Sometimes he carried his rifle and stopped to hunt along the way. He would arrive at a courthouse with the animal he had just shot hanging from his saddle.

Lawyers have to know the laws. They also have to be good speakers. A lawyer's job was to convince juries and judges that his clients were right. Patrick remembered the way Parson Davies had spoken when he was a boy. That's the way he talked to the juries. Patrick won a lot of cases, but they did not make him famous and rich.

Both parsons and tobacco had been very important in Patrick's life so far. Both parsons and tobacco were involved in the one case that would make him famous. It was called the Parsons' Cause.

The law said the parsons of the Episcopal churches were to be paid. The people who made the law wanted to be sure the parsons always had money to take care of their families. The law went on to say that the parsons were to be paid with tobacco.

Parsons weren't the only people paid in tobacco. At the time, tobacco was as good as money in Virginia. People didn't carry tobacco around in their pockets. Planters stored their huge tobacco leaves in storehouses. They received a slip of paper saying how much tobacco they had stored. When they bought something they gave the other person the slip of paper for the tobacco instead of money.

One year there was not much rain, so very little tobacco was harvested. The tobacco planters said they could not afford to give the parsons as much tobacco as the law said. The Virginia lawmakers wrote a new law. It said instead of giving the parsons tobacco, people could pay them two cents for each pound of tobacco they owed them.

The parsons didn't like this law at all. They knew tobacco sold for six cents a pound. The parsons thought they should be paid six cents a pound. King George in Britain agreed and **vetoed** the Virginia law.

Some parsons went to court to get more money. These were cases of the parsons against the people of Virginia. Patrick was hired to be

Workers load tobacco (in barrels, as seen on left) onto ships for delivery to Britain. In colonial Virginia, people were often paid in tobacco, which was as good as money at the time.

the people's lawyer for one of these cases.

Patrick was surprised when he rode up to the brick Hanover Courthouse. There were so many people crowded around the building that they couldn't all get inside. They stood outside in the December cold waiting to see what would happen.

Inside, people packed the oak benches.

More people squeezed along the walls. They plugged up the doorway. Everyone wanted to hear how much more money they would have to pay the parson.

Patrick had never spoken in front of such a large crowd of people. There were two people he wished weren't there. One was his uncle, Parson Henry. When Parson Henry's carriage stopped outside the courthouse, Patrick went out to talk to him. Patrick told him he wished he hadn't come.

"Why?" Parson Henry asked.

Patrick told him he would make him nervous. Then he wouldn't be able to do a good job for his clients.

Parson Henry left.

There was still one person in the courtroom who made Patrick nervous. Patrick couldn't ask him to leave. That was his father, Mr. Henry, the judge.

Only one parson was asking the court for more money that day. But over 20 other parsons sat together near Mr. Henry at the front of the room. They wanted to know how much more money the parson would get.

First the parson's lawyer spoke. Then it was time for Patrick to speak. He stood up. He looked at the floor. He slouched. He stuttered. He mumbled. He started sentences and didn't finish them.

The parsons gave each other sly looks. They thought the parson had already won.

The people watching hung their heads. They thought the parson had won, too. Mr. Henry slid down in his seat. He looked embarrassed because his son wasn't speaking very well.

Then Patrick realized the situation. He knew what he wanted to say. He knew how hard it was to grow tobacco. He had worked in the tobacco fields too. He knew that when the weather was bad there was very little harvest. He knew the poor farmers did not make very much money.

He stood up straight then. His blue eyes

Patrick Henry's dramatic speech in his first legal case, the Parson's Cause. Although he got off to a bad start, he finished with passion and won the case.

began to flash. His voice grew louder, steadier, stronger, and more determined.

Britain had given Virginia colonists the right to make their own tax laws, he reminded everyone. Why did King George think he knew better than the people living in Virginia how much they could afford to pay the parsons? Parsons should follow the law of Virginia.

People lifted their heads. They leaned as far forward as they could to listen carefully. Mr. Henry sat up straight again, looking a little less embarrassed.

Patrick's words grew braver. He said the king should not veto good laws. That wasn't protecting the people. The king was supposed to protect the people. If he didn't, people shouldn't have to obey him.

"**Treason**!" the other lawyer yelled, leaping to his feet. That meant he thought Patrick was an enemy of King George and Britain.

Patrick ignored him. He asked why the parsons were not feeding and clothing the poor people. Why were they trying to take more money from the poor, hard-working farmers, instead of helping them?

The parsons were extremely angry. They stood up and marched, stone-faced, straight out of the courtroom and the building.

The people watching were very excited and they showed it, hollering their approvals out loud. They'd never heard anyone speak so well. They said Patrick "made their blood run cold, and their hair to rise on end." Tears rolled down Mr. Henry's cheeks. He was proud of his son.

Patrick cleverly reminded the jury that they had to pay the parson *something*. It could be as little or as much as they wished.

It only took the jury a few minutes to make the decision. They decided the parson was to be paid in the amount of one penny.

The people cheered and threw their hats into the air. They lifted Patrick to their shoulders and carried him out into the courthouse yard.

The Parsons' Cause made Patrick Henry a well-known lawyer and speaker.

One man said, "Patrick, when he speaks, stirs the boys so that I've seen them jump up and crack their heels together, and slam their caps on the ground and stamp them."

Virginia and the other colonies needed a good speaker. Britain was about to make a law for a tax that would make the parsons' tax seem unimportant. It was called the Stamp Act.

The courthouse in Williamsburg, Virginia. In 1765 Patrick returned to Williamsburg to serve the colony of Virginia as an elected lawmaker, along with many other important men, in the House of Burgesses.

The King's Enemy?

The Parson's Cause made Patrick popular. People in Virginia liked him so much that they elected him to be a member of the Virginia **House of Burgesses,** a group of people chosen to make laws. So in May 1765 Patrick rode his horse over the clay roads again to Williamsburg.

He went to the building where the laws were made. It was shaped like a big H and was made of red bricks.

Patrick may have been nervous when he sat down with the other lawmakers. Most of them were rich men. They had been to college. They were the most powerful men in Virginia.

What were these important men talking about? A law to stop hogs from running loose in the town of Richmond! But the lawmakers soon moved on to more important things.

But Patrick didn't think they talked about the *most* important thing. He wanted to talk about Britain's new law, which was called the Stamp Act. He knew people in Virginia were unhappy with the law.

The Stamp Act said people must pay taxes on each business piece of paper. The paper would be stamped to show the tax was paid. Every kind of paper would be taxed–newspapers, wills, marriage certificates, and even decks of cards.

One night Patrick and three other lawmakers drew up a list of things they wanted to say. They called the list the Stamp Act **Resolutions**. The others asked Patrick to do the talking.

The next day was Patrick's 29th birthday, May 29, 1765. He stood up in the House of Burgesses and read the list. The list reminded the other lawmakers that Virginia had always made its own tax laws. Britain had taxed things it sold to Virginia before. But Britain had never made a law taxing things that people in Virginia sold to other people in Virginia.

Patrick agreed that Virginia and the other colonies in America were ruled by Britain. He said that the people living in the colonies were following the British laws. But no lawmakers in Britain were from the colonies. That was taxation without representation, which was against British law, so the Stamp Act was illegal under British law. Patrick went on to argue strongly that Virginians should only have to obey laws made by Virginia's lawmakers.

Some people who were loyal to Britain were angry at what Patrick said. "Treason! Treason!" they yelled.

The next day the Virginia lawmakers voted on the Stamp Act Resolutions. Twenty lawmakers agreed with Patrick; 19 did not. Many were still angry. Thomas Jefferson came from the college to listen to them argue. He said the arguments were "most bloody."

The *Virginia Gazette* printed the Resolutions. Newspapers in other colonies did too. Soon people in all the colonies were crying, "No taxation without representation!"

King George and the lawmakers in Britain kept the Stamp Act. They didn't like being told they couldn't tax the people in their colonies in America. The king also needed the money.

Britain had been fighting a long war with the French in America that had gone on for many years. They fought over who owned the land. The British persuaded some American Indian groups to help them fight the French. The French persuaded other Indian groups to help them fight against the British. The war was called the French and Indian War. The British had spent a lot of money fighting the war and when it was finally over, Britain was very deep in **debt**. The king had also sent many soldiers to live in the American colonies. The soldiers needed to be fed. Britain taxed the colonists to pay their war debts and feed their soldiers.

The colonists grew stubborn. Many decided not to buy anything from Britain. Then they wouldn't have to pay the tax. Instead they made as many things as they could.

Women promised not to buy cloth from Britain. They spun their own thread and yarn on spinning wheels. They had spinning parties. The women who spun the fastest and did the best work won prizes. At Patrick's home a loom was used to weave cloth. The cloth was made into clothes for his family and slaves.

In many cities and towns, men formed a secret club called the **Sons of Liberty**. They put up posters warning people not to sell Britain's tax stamps or use them. In many towns, the protesters were so angry they caught the tax collectors and tied them up on trees or "liberty poles." Sometimes they covered the tax collectors with sticky tar and feathers and chased them out of town.

Stamp tax collectors were sometimes tied up on "liberty poles" by angry colonists. Britain later repealed the Stamp Act.

Patrick Henry and other lawyers did not go to court anymore. They didn't want to pay taxes on their legal papers and have them stamped.

And everyone kept saying, "No taxation without representation!" Patrick was famous not only in Virginia. He was famous in all the American colonies. Wherever people met, they were sure to be talking about Patrick. He was the topic of conversation in stores, taverns, and churches.

Many important merchants in Britain were upset over the Stamp Act, too. They were losing a lot of money because people in America would not buy their goods. They asked the lawmakers in Britain to **repeal** the Stamp Act, so the British lawmakers did, saying the Stamp Act was no longer a law.

That made people in America happy. They rang church bells in every colony to celebrate.

More people than ever wanted Patrick as their lawyer. He worked very hard and made enough money to buy a nice new home for his family near Mount Brilliant. It was called Scotchtown. Patrick and Sallie needed a good-sized home because their family was growing.

There were lots of buildings at Scotchtown besides their house. There was a washhouse where the clothes were washed. Another small building was a summer kitchen where meals were made in the warm seasons so the house wouldn't get hot from the fireplace. There were stables for the horses and a smithy where a blacksmith made useful things for the farm. And there were houses for the many slaves.

Patrick wrote a letter to his daughter saying that her servants should be "well fed, well clothed, nursed in sickness, and let them never be unjustly treated." To someone else he wrote a letter saying that slavery was "evil." He said that he kept slaves due to the "[i]nconvenience of living without them; I will not, I cannot justify it." In his will he said his wife could "set free one or two" slaves if she wished.

Before long, people in America were very angry at Britain for yet another tax. This time the tax was on one of their favorite hot drinks, tea.

Patrick didn't like this new tax either. He went back to the House of Burgesses.

Thomas Jefferson was very disturbed by the new law too. He was also a burgess by that time.

Patrick and Thomas discussed the situation. They thought the colonists needed to know what laws were being made in Britain and what was happening in other colonies. They suggested that Virginia form a special committee to study all new British laws, then write letters about the laws and send them to the other colonies.

The others in the House of Burgesses liked the idea. They called the group of men the Committee of Correspondence. Patrick was asked to be on the first committee in Virginia.

News traveled slowly in the 1700s. There were no telephones or radios or televisions or computers. There were only a few newspapers. Sometimes it took weeks or months for people to find out important things that happened in other colonies or countries.

Patrick and the members of the Committee of Correspondence made sure that changed. They wrote down all the important things happening in Virginia. An **express rider** took the papers to the committees in other colonies. Those committees wrote back about the important things that happened in their own colonies.

The Virginia committee received bad news from Massachusetts. Three British ships loaded with tea had sailed into Boston Harbor. The Sons of Liberty didn't want the tea to be unloaded. However, the governor of Massachusetts wanted it brought ashore. He wouldn't let the ships leave Boston until all of the tea had been unloaded.

One night in December 1773 some of the Sons of Liberty decided to do something about that tea. They darkened their faces with grease and soot from lamps, so people wouldn't know who they were. Some dressed up to look like Indians. Then they climbed on board the three ships with the tea.

Their hatchets thunked against the wooden boxes. They dumped the tea out of the boxes and into the harbor. It took them more than three hours to unload 10,000 pounds of tea into the water. Then they left the ships without touching or damaging anything else.

British soldiers on parade in Boston. As punishment for the Boston Tea Party, the king sent more troops to close the port. This made people angry in all 13 colonies.

King George was furious when he heard about the event, which was called the Boston Tea Party. He ordered Boston Harbor closed until the people paid for the tea. He ordered that no ships could go in or out of Boston to bring food and supplies or do business. The king also sent more soldiers to stay in Boston. They were to make sure no ships were allowed to enter or leave the harbor.

People in all the colonies were upset. There had been English soldiers in the colonies for over 100 years. The soldiers had been there to help protect the colonists. At the time of the Boston Tea Party the soldiers weren't protecting the people. They were in Boston to force the colonists to do something they didn't want to do.

Patrick and Thomas Jefferson said it was time for people from each of the colonies to come together face-to-face to discuss events. The colonies all agreed and each sent **representatives** to a big meeting in Philadelphia called the Continental Congress. Two of the men from Virginia were Patrick and George Washington.

Men from Philadelphia met Patrick and George

Patrick Henry was called the Voice of the Revolution. He said what other people felt about Britain and liberty. He said things in a way that people remembered. Thomas Jefferson was called the Pen of the Revolution. He wrote the Declaration of Independence and many other important papers.

**George Washington as a young man.
George and Patrick were two of
Virginia's delegates to the first
Continental Congress in Philadelphia.**

Washington on the road six miles outside the
city. They paraded them into town with flutes
and drums. They were wild with excitement.

JOIN, or DIE.

Benjamin Franklin drew this cartoon showing the colonies as parts of a snake. The Continental Congress marked the first time the colonies worked together as one unit.

There had never been a meeting of people from all the colonies before. For the first time ever, the colonies were working together as one.

Patrick was the first speaker. He proclaimed, "The distinctions between Virginians, Pennsylvanians, New Yorkers, and New Englanders, are no more. I am not a Virginian, but an American!" He called for all colonies to join together against Britain.

What would they to do about the British soldiers and warships in Boston? The Congress discussed this in great detail, but they didn't have any clear answers.

It wasn't only the soldiers and taxes that worried them. The king of Britain had always appointed the colonies' governors. But the colonists elected their own sheriffs. Now King George said the governors would appoint the sheriffs. The sheriffs would decide who would be on juries. Colonists were afraid people wouldn't get fair trials.

The lawmakers couldn't meet in the House of Burgesses anymore because the governor of Virginia had closed it. He didn't like what the lawmakers were saying. Virginia's leaders decided they were going to meet anyway. This time they met in Richmond.

This happened to be a terribly sad time for

Patrick. His wife Sallie had been sick and she had just died. His six children needed him. But the meeting in Richmond was very important. What should he do?

Patrick took Patsy, his oldest daughter, aside and told her how important the meeting was. And he asked her to take care of the other children. Then he left for Richmond.

In Richmond there was no large government house for the lawmakers to meet in. Instead they met in a church. There were many people there. They wanted to know what the leaders would decide. People even stood outside and listened through the open windows. Patrick sat inside, in the third pew from the front.

Britain had sent more British soldiers and warships to the colonies since the meeting in Philadelphia. The king had told the soldiers to take all of the ammunition and cannons away from the towns. There was now the very real possibility of a war. Patrick thought something needed to be done.

He stood up to speak. If Virginia had its own army, Patrick said, Britain wouldn't have any reason to send soldiers to Virginia. If Britain didn't send soldiers, Britain wouldn't need to collect taxes to pay the soldiers.

Virginia's leaders argued over Patrick's idea. Some didn't think Virginia needed its own militia. Some argued that maybe the people in Boston should pay for the tea lost in the Boston Tea Party. Then King George wouldn't be angry anymore. Then the king would call the warships and soldiers back to Britain.

They knew Patrick wouldn't agree. When he stood up again, with that distinct look in his eyes, everyone stopped talking to listen.

Patrick Henry's famous speech to Virginia's lawmakers in Richmond. Patrick's dramatic words inspired people throughout the colonies to fight for freedom; two weeks later the Revolutionary War began.

"Give Me Liberty, or Give Me Death!"

Patrick's voice was calm when he started speaking. It didn't stay that way very long. Soon everyone in the church and everyone listening outside could hear him clearly. George Washington and Thomas Jefferson were there listening.

A parson who was there later recalled how Patrick's "voice rose louder and louder, until the walls of the building and all within them seemed to shake and rock."

What did Patrick say?

He started out saying that everyone hoped things would work out peacefully between Britain and the colonies. But he didn't think King George was going to forgive the colonies and let them have any peace.

"Does Britain have any enemies in the colonies to send armies and warships against?" Patrick asked out loud. He quickly answered his own question. "No, sir, she has none. They are meant for us."

He asked more questions. What could the colonists do about the armies and the other unfair things the king was doing to them? "Shall we try argument? Sir, we have been trying that for the last ten years. . . . There is no longer any room for hope."

Then he said the words that no one had dared to say before. "If we wish to be free . . . we must fight!"

"Gentlemen may cry peace, peace—but there is no peace. The war is actually begun!" The British soldiers had already closed Boston Harbor, and they were taking away all of the colonists' weapons and ammunition.

"Is life so dear or peace so sweet as to be purchased at the price of chains and slavery?" Patrick hunched over and bowed his head. He crossed his arms over his chest. He looked helpless, like a man tied up with heavy chains.

No one stirred. No one spoke. Everyone was sitting on the edge of their seats, holding their breath.

Suddenly, Patrick threw his head back sharply. He lifted his two clenched fists high over his head, as though they were bound by chains and bellowed, "Forbid it, Almighty God!"

How do we know for sure what Patrick Henry said? Many heroes of the American Revolution wrote down their speeches. Patrick Henry did not. People who heard him remembered what he said. Later some of them wrote down what they remembered, or told others who then wrote it down.

He bent over again, crossing his arms over his chest. He looked as though the chains were too heavy for him to stand up straight. "I know not what course others may take." He paused.

People leaned forward, staring at him.

Patrick straightened again. He lifted his chin

proudly. "But as for me, give me liberty!" He uncrossed his arms and thrust them back into the air. Then his left hand dropped to his side.

"Or give me death!" His right hand violently plunged to his chest in a fist, as though he were being stabbed.

No one said a word. They were stunned. Even the people who thought it was wrong to fight didn't say anything. They sat in silence and thought about what Patrick had just said.

After a few moments, Thomas Jefferson stood and said that he agreed with Patrick. Then another man, and another. The lawmakers agreed and voted to raise a militia in Virginia.

Within two weeks everyone knew Patrick was right. It was too late for peace. On April 19, 1775, the first battles of the Revolutionary War were fought. They were called the Battles of Lexington and Concord.

People in all the colonies heard about Patrick's passionate speech. They made up a song about it. Part of the song went:

The Battles of Lexington and Concord, the first battles of the Revolutionary War. Men, women, and children throughout the colonies were now at war with Britain.

Each free-born Briton's song should be,
Or give me death or Liberty.

Patrick was made leader of the Virginia militia. The newly formed group of colonists-turned-soldiers was called Culpepper's Company. They wore green shirts with white letters on them that read "Liberty or Death." Many of them paid dearly for the new country's liberty with their lives.

Some people thought Patrick wasn't the best army leader. They thought the militia needed a leader who knew more about being an officer. Patrick left the army because of this.

Many men had joined the militia because Patrick was their leader. They were mad when they were given another leader. Patrick didn't like it either. But he believed the things they were fighting for were more important than his feelings. He went from tent to tent, talking to the soldiers. He asked them to stay and fight for their rights. And they did.

Patrick couldn't keep fighting as a soldier, but he fought in other ways. The governor of Virginia had left and Virginia needed a new one. For the first time people could vote for the person they wanted to be the governor.

They voted for Patrick. He was so popular that he served five terms. Each term was one year long.

While he was governor, he remarried. His

new wife's name was Dorothea. Patrick called her Dolly. She was 21 years old. Dolly and George Washington's wife, Martha, were cousins.

The Revolutionary War went on for many years. It finally ended in 1783.

After the war, a new country was formed. It was named the United States of America. The name told other countries that many states agreed to be joined together and to work together.

The first time Patrick met Thomas Jefferson was at Dorothea's parents' house when Patrick and Thomas attended a Christmas party there. At the time Dorothea was only a little girl.

There was a lot of work to be done for the new country. The United States had to have its own laws. Patrick was one of the people chosen to help make the laws. The laws would be called the Constitution of the United States.

When the Constitution was finally passed by the Congress, Patrick was not entirely happy with it. He thought the Constitution took too much power away from the states.

Representatives from the 13 states sign the Constitution. Three years later, thanks to Patrick's efforts, the Bill of Rights was added to the Constitution.

The Constitution didn't include many of the people's rights that Patrick and others thought it should. He wanted it to say that people have a right to say what they believe, even things about their leaders. He also wanted it to say that newspapers have a right to print what they want, and that people can worship God however they choose.

Patrick and his friends came up with a list of people's rights. It was called the Bill of Rights.

There were some leaders who liked the Constitution but didn't like the Bill of Rights. They said the Constitution was fine just the way it was written.

All of the states had to **ratify**, or vote "yes" to, the Constitution. Until they did, it would not be the law of the United States. Patrick asked other Virginia leaders not to vote for the Constitution until a Bill of Rights was added. He wanted to make sure no one could ever take people's rights away in America again, the way King George had tried to do with the colonists.

Patrick often used the words liberty and freedom in his speeches. He thought liberty was "the greatest of all earthly blessings."

"Something must be done to preserve your liberty and mine," he said. "I speak as one poor individual, but when I speak, I speak the language of thousands." He meant that thousands of people agreed with him.

One day while Patrick was speaking, the room grew darker and darker. The thick clouds shut out the sun. Patrick kept speaking. He told the other Virginia leaders that the Constitution was dangerous without a Bill of Rights. "I see it. I feel it," he said. It seemed that Heaven was watching what choices the leaders made.

Crash! A great clap of thunder and a bright flash of lightening startled the listeners. Rain came pouring down. The violent storm was so loud that people couldn't even hear Patrick speak. Some listeners thought it was like Heaven talking to them.

Finally it was time for the leaders to vote. Would they agree with Patrick? Would they say there must be a Bill of Rights before they agreed to make the Constitution law in Virginia?

The leaders stood up and formed two lines. The people watching leaned over the balcony to count them. The leaders voting "yes" stood in one line. The leaders voting "no" stood in the other. The lines looked the same length.

The leaders stayed in their lines and walked slowly through the door. The doorkeepers counted how many men were in each line. There were 80 leaders in the "yes" line. There were 88 leaders in the "no" line.

George Washington once said Patrick "has only to say let this be Law, and it is Law." But this time, what Patrick wanted did not become law. Not right away.

Patrick did not give up. He kept asking many different representatives of Congress, over and over again, to add a Bill of Rights to the Constitution. Three years later, Congress did.

Was Patrick really lazy? Patrick and Thomas Jefferson started out as friends. They worked together for the colonies before and during the Revolutionary War. Patrick was Virginia's first elected governor. Thomas was the second. Patrick didn't like some things Jefferson did as governor. That made Thomas mad. When Thomas was old, he wrote that Patrick was lazy, uneducated, and not a good lawyer. Maybe Thomas believed these things, but they weren't true. Patrick had worked his way up from a poor man to a lawyer. He took more than 1,000 cases in three years and won most of them.

Patrick Henry in later life. Although President George Washington wanted him to take several government jobs, Patrick said no. He was happy to stay home with his family at Red Hill.

Grandfather Patrick

People wanted Patrick to keep working as a
leader. George Washington was elected the
first president of the United States. The president
asked Patrick to take many important jobs. Patrick
said no to each one of them. He wanted to stay
home with his family. They had moved again. Their
new home was called Red Hill.

Patrick had many children. He and his first
wife, Sallie, had six: Martha (called Patsy), John,
Anne, Elizabeth, William, and Edward (called
Neddy). They all grew up and had children of their
own. Three of Patrick and Sallie's children died

before Patrick did.

Patrick and Dolly had 11 children: Dorothea (also called Dolly), Sarah (called Sallie), Martha Catherine, Patrick, Fayette, Alexander Spotswood, Nathaniel, Richard, Jane Robertson, Edward Winston, and John. Richard and Jane Robertson died as babies. John was only three years old when Patrick died.

Patrick loved his children and grandchildren. One friend said, "His visitors have not infrequently caught him lying on the floor, with a group of these little ones climbing over him in every direction, or dancing around him with . . . mirth, to the tune of his violin, while the only contest seemed to be who should make the most noise."

Patrick's young sons went "bareheaded, barefooted, hallooing and whooping about the plantation in every direction."

Patrick's great-granddaughter said about him, "He was greatly attached to his children, whom he treated as companions and friends."

On June 6, 1799, Patrick died at Red Hill.

A copy of the Stamp Act Resolutions was found with his will. Patrick had written on the back, "Whether this will prove a blessing or a curse, will depend upon the use our people make of the blessings which a gracious God hath bestowed on us."

Your life and mine would have been very different if Patrick Henry hadn't worked for people's rights and freedoms, and fought for them with his voice.

GLOSSARY

cicadas–large insects, common in the summer, that make buzzing or chirping sounds by rubbing body parts together

colony–an area controlled by a distant country

debt–money or things owed

dowry–a gift of goods or money that a bride's father gives to the groom

Episcopal–a type of Christian church similar to the Church of England

express rider–a person who carried messages by horseback

fine–money paid for breaking a law

House of Burgesses–a group of people who made laws in Virginia; also the place they met

militia–a group of civilian men called into the military only during emergencies

muster–gather together

parson–a pastor, or clergyman, in a Christian church

plantation–a large estate that grows mainly one crop for sale

ratify–the process a group uses to approve a document

repeal–to do away with or discontinue a law

representative–a leader elected by the people to serve in government

resolution–a formal statement

Sons of Liberty–a group of people organized to fight for freedom for the colonies

treason–betraying your country or giving secrets to the enemy

veto–a leader's power to refuse to let something become a law

CHRONOLOGY

1736   Patrick Henry born on May 29.

1754   Marries 16-year-old Sarah Shelton.

1760   Becomes a lawyer.

1763   Fights against the Parsons' Cause and makes his first great speech.

1765   Becomes a member of the Virginia House of Burgesses; speaks against Stamp Act; Stamp Act Resolutions passed.

1773   Recommends, along with Thomas Jefferson, the formation of the first Virginia Committee of Correspondence.

1775   First wife, Sarah, dies; makes "Give Me Liberty or Give Me Death" speech on March 23.

1776   Elected governor of Virginia for the first time.

1777   Marries Dorothea "Dolly" Dandridge.

1788   Argues against the Constitution; proposes the Bill of Rights.

1791   The Bill of Rights is passed.

1799   Dies on June 6 at age 63.

REVOLUTIONARY WAR TIME LINE

1765   The Stamp Act is passed by the British. Violent protests against it break out in the colonies.

1766   Britain ends the Stamp Act.

1767   Britain passes a law that taxes glass, painter's lead, paper, and tea in the colonies.

1770   Five colonists are killed by British soldiers in the Boston Massacre.

1773   People are angry about the taxes on tea. They throw boxes of tea from ships in Boston harbor into the water. It ruins the tea. The event is called the Boston Tea Party.

1774   The British pass laws to punish Boston for the Boston Tea Party. They close Boston harbor. Leaders in the colonies meet to plan a response to these actions.

1775   The battles of Lexington and Concord begin the American Revolution.

1776   The Declaration of Independence is signed. France and Spain give money to help the Americans fight Britain. Nathan Hale is captured by the British. He is charged with being a spy and is executed.

1777   Leaders choose a flag for America. The American troops win some important battles over the British. General Washington and his troops spend a very cold, hungry winter in Valley Forge.

1778 France sends ships to help the Americans win the war. The British are forced to leave Philadelphia.

1779 French ships head back to France. The French support the Americans in other ways.

1780 Americans discover that Benedict Arnold is a traitor. He escapes to the British. Major battles take place in North and South Carolina.

1781 The British surrender at Yorktown.

1783 A peace treaty is signed in France. British troops leave New York.

1787 The U.S. Constitution is written. Delaware becomes the first state in the Union.

1789 George Washington becomes the first president. John Adams is vice president.

FURTHER READING

Barner, Bob. *Which Way to the Revolution? A Book About Maps.* New York: Holiday House, 1998.

Fritz, Jean. *Where Was Patrick Henry on the 29th of May?* New York: Coward-McCann, 1975.

Glubok, Shirley. *Home and Child Life in Colonial Days.* New York: Macmillan, 1969.

Gross, Ruth Belov. *If You Grew Up with George Washington.* New York: Scholastic, 1993.

Reische, Diana. *Patrick Henry.* New York: Franklin Watts, 1987.

Tyler, Moses Coit. *Patrick Henry.* Boston: Houghton Mifflin, 1887. Reprint: New York: Chelsea House, 1980.

INDEX

PICTURE CREDITS

page

3: The Library of Congress
6: Stokes Collection/Print Division/
    The New York Public Library
11: Picture Collection/The New York
    Public Library
15: Stokes Collection/Print Division/
    The New York Public Library
16: Picture Collection/The New York
    Public Library
21: The Library of Congress
22: Picture Collection/The New York
    Public Library
24: Picture Collection/The New York
    Public Library
27: The Library of Congress

31: National Archives
34: Picture Collection/The New York
    Public Library
38: The Library of Congress
44: National Archives
49: Picture Collection/The New York
    Public Library
51: The Library of Congress
52: The Library of Congress
56: National Archives
61: National Archives
64: National Archives
68: Picture Collection/The New York
    Public Library

ABOUT THE AUTHOR

JOANN A. GROTE loves to read and write about history. She has written over 20 historical novels for adults and children. Her short stories and articles have been published in magazines including *'Teen* and *Guideposts for Kids.* JoAnn worked at the historical restoration of Old Salem in Winston-Salem, North Carolina, for five years. Today she lives in Minnesota.

Senior Consulting Editor **ARTHUR M. SCHLESINGER, JR.** is the leading American historian of our time. He won the Pulitzer Prize for his book *The Age of Jackson* (1945), and again for *A Thousand Days* (1965). This chronicle of the Kennedy Administration also won a National Book Award. He has written many other books, including a multi-volume series, *The Age of Roosevelt.* Professor Schlesinger is the Albert Schweitzer Professor of the Humanities at the City University of New York, and has been involved in several other Chelsea House projects, including the Colonial Leaders series of biographies on the most prominent figures of early American history.